Thought-Apples

Thought-Apples

25 Poems

Bert Flitcroft

Offa's Press
2017

First published in 2014 by Offa's Press,
Ferndale, Pant, Oswestry, Shropshire, SY10 9QD.

Reprinted in 2017

ISBN: 978-0-9565518-7-0

Designed, printed and bound by Lion FPG Limited,
Oldbury Road, West Bromwich, B70 9DQ.

Contents

Acknowledgements: Waiting for Anna appeared in the *Warwick Review*, Forget Gravity and Mevagissey Harbour appeared in the anthology *We're All in This Together*, Offa's Press, 2012.

It's all in...

It is still possible, you know,
in your granddad years,
to 'cut the mustard' on the dance floor;
to meet head-on the thrill, the dangers
of pulling a sled across the ice pack
or crossing the Himalayas in a balloon
with an iron lung strapped to your back.

To re-discover the challenge of geometry,
the hinterland of trigonometry,
the sheer reverberations of Pythagoras.
To taste afresh the language of triangles:
sine and cosine, isosceles and equilateral,
the square on the hypotenuse.

To learn, late on, that an egg has mass
and therefore it must have gravity.
That I have mass, and therefore gravity.
That between us the egg and I, in theory,
could tilt the north face of the Eiger.

That if two marbles were left
either end of a horizontal, air-smooth table,
in a hundred thousand years or more
they would eventually meet and kiss.
And it would be the longest kiss of all time.

Still going on

In the High Street they are toe to toe,
shouting, their shadows boxing.
She is a harpy jabbing at his chest,
her voice polluting the hanging baskets.
How can they be so oblivious?
I am not here.
A woman in green does not walk by.
The sun is cold between them.

Later, in the park, I pass them at a table.
He is sideways on, hunched and reading,
his eyes two hurricanes of concentration.
She is scribbling, then lifts her head,
flicks a greenfly from her forearm,
applies a layer of lip balm and looks away.
The sun is still cold between them.
A thrush bashes a snail against a stone.

Forget gravity

They say that love is everything,
those who know that you can die from it.

Wouldn't it be something, to discover
that the driving force behind the universe,
behind every patch of red or purple gas
where matter is still forming, was love.

That planets hang around together
because they love each other,
like particles of passion holding hands
in a reverie of inexplicable black holes.

Wouldn't it be something, some sort of comfort,
to know that in every nook and cranny of the stars
this force - nebulous, excited to self-luminosity,
bright as the spiral of Andromeda

but insubstantial as Magellan's clouds* -
will in the end always coalesce,
shape itself out in the dark into a ring,
a single glass of wine, an empty chair?

* two small starry nebulae, visible
  from the Southern hemisphere.

Head over heels

Why do we talk of 'falling',
of being head-over-heels,
when we're in the first throes of love,
as if on a downward spiral
that's bound to end in disaster?

It would make more sense
to talk of rising.
Some do climb into it
as if mounting a step ladder
to change a light bulb,
or stepping onto an elevator
while looking down at their feet.
Others allow themselves to float
away on a rising balloon
carried wherever by the wind.
Some of us, like all great lovers,
can't help ourselves. We
fearlessly
shin up the ivy
just because it's there.

S.P.A.D. *

Shunted together by chance in the clank
and steam of a Midlands railway town,
two teenagers at grammar school.
One head one heart, too clever
for the boiler suits behind the pantry door.

He kept their lives on track:
stability, the kids, the family home, all that,
and a house full of books,
their titles placed
to face into the rooms
like semaphores.

On track, until the morning she tidied
away the ironing, the marmalade,
and sat with the wedding album -
the two of them cutting the cake,
looking up at the camera.
First love.
Such black-and-white beginnings.

And reading signals can be difficult.
So many junctions, so many destinations.
Until that morning, when she slapped
the album shut,
hoovered up her yesterdays,
uncoupled   from that sense of loss
that lifelong marriages can bring,
and, passing a red, pulled out of the sidings.

* Signal passed at danger

Little ways

She hangs jumpers out spread-eagled
over four lines of the whirligig
to stop them stretching, pegged
under the arms at the seam.
She's so particular.
She lets dishes drip at lunchtime in the rack
on top of those already dry.
So careless.
The beds are aired daily
with duvets and sheets folded back,
creaseless in apple-pie formation.
So meticulous.
At bedtime the daily paper is left
open on the floor, crossword up.
It's so annoying.
And she walks from room to room
with a toothbrush foaming from her mouth
as if to save time.

I don't know what I do.
Something with pots and pans, I think,
or closing the curtains badly, perhaps.
Certainly, singing the first line of a song
without thinking, for weeks on end.
But other things?
I don't know, and I don't ask,
and she doesn't say.
It would be like moaning,
which we try not to do.

Pouring oil

I have offered myself up to the soft slab
like a sacrificial lamb.
She is silking warm oil with the softest palms,
up my xylophone ribs in practised lines,
between boulders of shoulders, from side to side.

We have said hello, made our small talk
and now we have drifted into silence.
Neither of us is present.
I'm drifting away to the sound of waves
kissing and hushing the shingle.
She is somewhere listening to skylarks.

Then, out of the blue, she mutters
'Bloody marriage. Bloody men.'
And the silence returns.

And I'm a newly-wed again,
under your tender hands
with candles and sandalwood
scenting a half-lit room.
And I'm thinking of deeper water
beneath the silence.
Has she poured oil of Cedar, I wonder,
on their troubled walks,
soothed with sandalwood their pillow talks,
paid attention to the knots?

The Secret?

To a stoat, running down its prey,
a rabbit must be just another rabbit.
A cow with its head between the bars
is not longing for the taste of artichoke.
A tree, let's say a beech, does not dream
of waking in a different field.

                Their expectation is sameness.

Though we have moulded to each other,
meeting and passing like a pair of badgers
snuffling in their set,

                we treasure difference:

a moose, stripping branches by the roadside,
a pheasant, pecking at the picture window,
the smokiness of Lapsang on a Sunday.

So tell me, are my sagging jowls,
my gunny sack of worn-out jokes,
the way I fail to close the curtains,

                a sameness, or a difference?

And is that the secret? I'd like to know.

To a polite audience at a poetry reading
in a public garden

It could be a lovely way to spend an hour,
admiring blue delphiniums spread like stars
and planets of globe thistles swaying
in their own infinity of space.

But why exactly are you standing there, listening
to some self-appointed poet eulogising
over the perfection of red blighted roses,
comparing dragonflies to baseball bats?

Are you that keen to hear his dysfunctional brain
comparing the moon to an old sock,
his love to a tortoise in the long grass
or his life to a ball of garden string, unwinding?

You may understand the sub-text of a spud growing
in the dark, swelling beneath the soil,
or parsnips forking as they wait for the cold,
but really I know you're waiting for the reading to end,

in sympathy with the downtrodden worms
burrowing deeper as the poems rain down on them.
And look, there's a local snail retreating into his shell
with his hands over his ears.

Forbidden fruit

There must be clusters of people around the world:
    orchard keepers, cider makers, pastry chefs,
        who are fanatical about apples.

But I'm not one of them. I'm struggling
    to write a poem about apples,
        to wax lyrical about sin or their skins,

although I'm sure there is a complete lexicon
    of apples any fool can research. Dwarfs,
        half-standard, pippins, come to mind.

I simply am not moved by an apple,
    no more than I am moved by a courgette
        or a piano stool or sets of teaspoons.

So I am sitting idly with my pen, waiting,
    and a thought comes, and the thought is a question.
        What if our thoughts were really apples?

Then we are all walking round full of apples,
    our branches weighed down with fruit,
        most of it unripe or too sweet or too sharp to bite into.

And so these apple-thoughts remain unpicked,
    destined to drop un-tasted by the world,
        left scattered on the grass like wasted windfalls.

Waiting for Anna

This Moses basket fresh by the bed
is waiting,
like a promise, like a Truth
about to come true.
Not for a casting off among the reeds
but for a coming
home.

To open a door, to enter a room,
is always to begin again.
Already the basket's empty space,
the very air inside it,
is sacred.
There is nothing more to say.
Silence has a voice.
Emptiness is eloquent.

Seal of approval

Just someone's ordinary children,
up there on the stage
like unknown continents,
shaking hands, their gowns
like bright red ticks of approval.
Doctors.
It was all a bit surreal,
difficult to pin down.

What were we thinking?
Not much, I guess, at the time.
Too busy with pride.

It was only much later, years,
that I really saw it.
The good they would do.
The lives they would save.
The enormity of it.

Who would have thought?
So young.
Just someone's ordinary children.

Human Geography

'Somewhere north there's been a fatality,'
we're told. That's it. Nothing else.
Nothing about a trespasser
or cyclist smashed at a level crossing.

Up the line men in jumpsuits are scooping up
remnants of a corpse from the blackened ballast,
striding the sleepers hunting for an arm
and left leg in the rosebay willow herb.

To the south, in Birmingham, clerks are computing
slots through New Street,
new routes looping east and west
to by-pass the problem.
Meanwhile trains are backing up
north and south
like morse-code signals
at stubborn lights, as red as fresh blood,
on rails flexing under their dead weight.

Here, on the platform, there are mutterings.
Sparrows flit about.
What we don't see doesn't touch us.
Outside Sheffield a driver is re-living
the bump, feeling over and over
the hint of a shudder rising through his bones.
He knows about the nightmares to come,
will see over and over the face and staring eyes.
He will see the sudden plummet into grief,
in a terraced house
somewhere south of Dronfield.

Rage on the M42

I was following the rules. Why couldn't he?
The signs said 50, clear and glowing
poppy red inside a halo of white spots
he couldn't miss. Four lurid circles!

The thrust of his bonnet, that badge,
his number plate with engorged letters
K1NG, entitle him to nothing –
no special dispensation from the Pope,
the Queen, the Minister of Transport.
Floating along on his six-litre cloud,
his fat backside leather- bound,
his nose in the air, tacking in and out
between the rest of us mere mortals.

I was following the rules. Why couldn't he?
I cursed his arrogance, his ball-bearings,
the smoothness of his ride.
I prayed, 'Please God, let him puncture a tyre.
Make him scrabble around for the jack,
get oil on his cuffs, lie down in the dirt.
Make his wheels - all the circles
of his life - turn for ever into squares.'

Central Park, Sunday

The city is sloughing off the week.
Somewhere deep in the Park,
among the meandering pedals, the joggers,

the strollers, the picnics and young love
lying with its ankles crossed,
a clown is conjuring bubbles

with a length of thick rope. We pause
to watch a globe inhale into pregnancy,
stretch out into a slug, become a whale,

distend into a buffalo,
until the sheen of its haunches
can bear the tension no longer.

The sigh of disappointment is audible.
He is selling sculpture, not himself.
A knot of Japanese bends down

to place ten-dollar notes
into his battered doctor's bag.
There is so little magic in the world.

Saturdays

He is late and she will be waiting
as he heads due south with the idlers and lorries,
the rush of coaches and crush of vans.
Soon he will skirt the whirlpool of the roundabout
and broach the green and in-between places,
ticking off the ancient landmarks of *Kings
and Farthings, Bull's Heads* and *Butlers Arms.*
By now she'll be impatient, her life reduced
to the spotlight of her own existence,
drumming her fingers on the arm of the settee.

He decides to take his time, to dawdle
past *The Highwayman,* remembering the moors
and moons and clouds of ghostly galleons,
before he enters the suddenness of suburb
with its politeness of traffic and bay windows,
a slowing down of thirties in red circles,
the familiar thin blue line of well-behaved,
tidy waste disposal bins and boxes.
At the run of uncooperative lights he is content
to pause, to tap along with the Ronettes
while an elderly couple inch across the zebra.
Soon he will swing into the drive,
nonchalantly wave the key in the air,
watch the yellow lights wink goodbye,
and turn to see her face, stern at the window.

Naked

My auntie Lizzie, the one with the big hair,
once told my mother that her second husband
Reg, the one with the thin legs,
liked to walk round the house naked.
She shuddered at the thought of it.

Perhaps they thought
I was too young to understand.
I suppose I was.
It came back to me this morning,
standing in the bathroom shaving.

Walking with arthritis

The brain is working well enough.
The odd forgetful moment, perhaps:
'Where did I put that spoon?' Or
'What does parataxis mean?' I demand of it.
'Bang bang!' I say, to shock it into action,
and hold two fingers to my temple.

The fingers still flex, at least. I can hold
a cold fish, cup my wife's warm breasts.
It's just the knees. They bend
and bear the weight but complain
in foreign tongues, speak the language
of Meniscus the Greek philosopher,
or Cartilage that roguish Roman emperor.
Sometimes it's Bursar, the moneylender.

Whole treatises have been written,
poems penned, in praise of knees
but I cannot find it in me to wax lyrical.
This time it's personal.
You cannot tell a leg not to limp, it doesn't work,
nor thrust a hill away behind you.
Overnight I've become a walking apology
to fellow ramblers, the knees
no longer udder-soft or pliable.

There is a mystery to life, some say

I do not need philosophers or priests to tell me so,
for I have climbed and rambled where the walkers go:
Cat Bells, Skiddaw, the Dales, the Chase,
Red Pike, the grit-stone face of Froggatt Edge.

With every climb there is a sense of leaving
behind. Not of the grieving kind,
for it touches something natural in man
to be outdoors and seeking higher ground,
to open the gate that leaves the road behind.

Rather, it is a finding, a reminding
of the grandeur of green and open space,
and cloud-cottoned heights that touch steep skies,
where the larks and the lapwings weave
you into the natural scheme of things.

And always there is a looking down.
To see a lane meandering along the valley floor,
the tiny sheepdog in his yard,
the farmhouse you can blot out with your thumb,
is to come to see yourself, to know
and to enjoy your littleness.

I smile when I remember
a certain rock to perch on, a spot beneath a tree,
a view where, by sitting still,
we begin to own it and are part of it.
And I think of climbing such a hill
or treading such a path, not as a going
but a kind of coming home,
a threshold crossed, a knowing
that such a place, once owned, cannot be lost.

Pièta

I was ten when I discovered I was C.of E.
accepted birth control, it seemed,
and all things bright and beautiful.
There are memories of dad kneeling
with his big, veined hands together
and Sunday school in a thunderstorm,
and a scattering of funerals making God
a more important word than table or chair.

Until, much older, the Pièta – figures
carved into a church wall, recessed
and half-hidden in the shadows;
shades of a father in corduroy comforting
a teenage son draped across his knees.
Not a conversion – more a glimpse,
an opening sentence promising more.
Some things you have to be ready for.

New City Library.

Outside she is sharp-edged; wears a dress
of boxes sequined with wedding rings,
as if Picasso had cat-walked her outfit
out of his imagination into ours.

By contrast he is formal, all white suit,
erect and, for the fashion-conscious, braced
with Doric pillars, finished off with marble shoes.
Traditional. Solid. Safe as a bank.

Cheek by jowl, but slightly aloof,
they seem at first an ill-matched pair.
Yet side by side they set each other off,
their virtues heightened by the difference.

Ideally suited some would say. Odd couples
can make the happiest marriages.

St. Cuthbert's Way

His thin fingers stroke the sliver of wood,
feel its familiar grain, its tapering point.
What matters is the hunger, the pains,
the shivering, these raw blistered feet.
He would savour them, rejoice
in the union of flesh and sharp stone.

Climbing, he butts up against a wall,
a barrier that makes the bracken-bending,
heather-slicing wind growl with anger,
a wolf-hound warning off intruders.
Legs taut as springs he jumps,
his eyes like two brown pebbles, searching.

Such a long, long journey, over years of miles.
He knows that where the sun comes up
must be the sea, the island described in stories
by the wretched with their hovels and pigs.
There he will find a space he can fill, build
a stronghold for the new teachings.

His thin fingers stroke the sliver of wood,
feel its familiar grain, its tapering point.
He hesitates, sniffs the wind and listens.
He howls a question down the valley,
begins to pad towards the sheep-skull clouds
to find that breach in the wall.

This place

This narrow strip of Staffordshire
I think of as the county's lowlands,
where the gods decided rock and moor
should be ironed out, flat as a glide in the Trent,
left damp as a riverside mist at dawn.
Here wind is free to race across the fields,
to whistle through thin hedgerows, dip
into ditches to ruffle stagnant wet.

This place is frontier land.
Danes rowed up with dragons at their heads.
Normans settled for the waterside.
Now and then a groat will open its dull eyes,
sesterces will blink in the sudden daylight.
Rome marched and garrisoned here.
They understood a road is more than just a road.
It is a presence, a dividing line, a sword thrust.

And here Rykneld Street is still a shield wall.
To the west of it a line of settlements
are strung out like laundry:
a 'tun', a 'wood', a 'wash', a 'ley', a 'field'
drying out among the alders and tall poplars,
spires and mulched villages that crouch
in the blanched season waiting to open their doors
to the warmth of warblers and hovering damselflies.

But to the east a rash of quarries like shingles scabs
scour and rape the earth for pebbles and gravel,
following a seam of hard-core ballast,
littering the land with mounds and deep sinks,
leaving water havens for wild fowl where holes -
you cannot call them lakes –
have filled themselves like blisters.
Winter swans leave when they can.

Mevagissey harbour: August

The seagulls have stopped jeering,
have fallen silent over the jade glass.
Orange flags, taut and quivering
in the offshore wind, are pointing out to sea.
Sunhats have shoaled into the dripping cafes,
waiting it out with tea and cherry scones.
The rain is slanting down.

A couple hunch out to the end of the jetty
seeking a reason for being there,
to have the sea on three sides,
leaning over the rail to peer into the depths;
to feel the swell in their bones;
to wonder how they would cope if they fell in.
The rain is slanting down.

Across the harbour entrance a Labrador
looking for fun and bones
pads out to the end, stops at the sharp drop
and peers out over the water,
his doggy brain trying to make sense of it all:
the white horses, the tiny spike of a lighthouse,
the rain slanting down.

Behind him the harbour wall is left deserted.
The picket line of fishermen have stopped lobbing
out their lead weights and lines of feathers,
leaving the clouds of mackerel and pollack in peace.
On the hillside a jumble of cottages
paints a pastel waterfall.
The rain is slanting down.

What I know

What I heard, was the sound of a stumble,
the grunt and gasp of human calamity,
the dead-weight thud of a body
toppling like a bag of onions
against a heavy door.

What I saw, was an ageing man
with gravy-stains across his trousers
prone across the doorstep of a bank,
his legs askew like awkward children.
And a couple crossing over, arms outstretched
like two descending angels
clutching Marks and Spencers shopping bags.

What I know, is the shock
at seeing someone slump in the street,
butting up against the animality of life.
That your heart and kidneys have no conscience,
your lungs show no remorse.
That your body is destined to let you down.

That tomorrow I could pop out to the shops,
shout through to my wife, 'I'll be back soon,'
leave her in the kitchen baking bread,
and never return.

That it could happen this afternoon.
That only this cafe's red-check table cloth,
this sticky toffee pudding, the spoon in my hand,
is real.